HOW TO PAY OFF YOUR MORTGAGE 4-12 YEARS SOONER

AND SAVE TENS OF THOUSANDS IN INTEREST

JAKE TAYLOR

Jacobs & Whitehall
73-03 Bell Blvd, #10
Oakland Gardens, NY 11364
www.jacobsandwhitehall.com
Tel: (888) 991-2766

Quantity sales: Special discounts are available on quantity purchases by corporations, associations, and others. For details, contact the publisher at the address above.
Printed in the United States of America

Published in 2020

ISBN: 978-1-951149-52-9

Dedication

Although it may seem hopeless at first, or the beginning of a never-ending road, you CAN pay off your mortgage, even a few years sooner than you think, without a tremendous effort.

Once you pay off your mortgage and discover how to save yourself years of time and tens of thousands of interest payments, you're going to feel the wind of financial freedom pushing you forward towards a prosperous future.

This book is dedicated to the American Dream, and the dream of owning your home free and clear.

DISCLAIMER

This publication is intended to be used for educational purposes only. No legal advice is being given, and no attorney-client, lender-client, broker-client, or fiduciary relationship is created by reading this material. The author, publisher, and any associated persons or entities assume no liability for errors, omissions or how this book or its contents are used or interpreted, or for any consequences resulting directly or indirectly from the use of this book. For legal or any other advice, please consult an experienced attorney or the appropriate professional, who may be more aware of your personal and business circumstances and the laws in your jurisdiction.

Pilot Mortgage, LLC
727 W. Ray Rd #B7
Gilbert, AZ
(480) 999-3339
www.JakeTaylor.com

What Clients Say About Jake Taylor and Pilot Mortgage

"Jake Taylor and his team at Pilot Mortgage are hands down the best! I have bought 7 houses and used big banks, and other mortgage brokers and they were ok at best. Jake's customer service is on a whole different level. He takes time to explain the best options and ways to save money. I once received a call out of the blue from Jake and he explained how he could refinance my house and save me thousands of dollars. I have referred my Mom, dad, brother, and many close friends to Jake over the years and will continue to do so. I don't even bother calling other companies anymore because I know Jake will get me the best rates possible. Thank you, Jake, for always looking out for me and my family."

– *Adam Miller*

****

"I have now used Jake to refinance my home and to purchase a home. He was extremely patient and helpful during the loan process. Both times I used Jake, he did an amazing job of explaining all my loan options. Without any pressure, he helped me make the decisions that were in my best interest. He was able to secure the best rates possible for my mortgages. I highly recommend using Jake for your mortgage needs. I will definitely be using him again in the future."

— *Stephen Hale*

****

"You will not find a better broker that works harder for you. I can count on Jake and his team to tell me the truth and the loans they provide are phenomenal. They explain things in a way I can understand and they have amazing competitive rates. I highly recommend The Jake Taylor team at Pilot mortgage."

– Nicole Brown

****

"I wanted to take a moment on behalf of my husband and myself to thank Jake Taylor and his team at PILOT Mortgage from the bottom of our hearts for ALL your help, and for covering the fees for the lock extension. We appreciate it beyond words and have to tell you that this was the EASIEST process I have ever gone through, with the least amount of stress, and with the best customer service from start to finish by you both, as well as Carrie, who has been an angel! :) I will be highly recommending you to anyone I hear of wanting to purchase a home or refinance. Thanks again for everything!!! You guys were amazing!!!!"

– Judy Laufer

****

"I highly recommend Jake he made my refinancing so easy and fast in less than 30 days I'm now waiting for my close date. He always answered my texts and questions right away which was super important to me to receive answers timely since customer service is so important to me. Very happy customer!!"

– Debbie Ashton

****

Absolutely the best lender experience I have ever had. I am so glad that I ended up with Jake Taylor as I felt he had my best interests in mind throughout the entire process. He is very friendly and easy to work with and talk to. He makes sure you have a solid understanding of the process and everything going on. Best of all, he works fast!!! Jake was able to complete my entire loan process, including underwriting in just 4 DAYS!!! That is incredible!! Depending on the house I went with I could have closed in 10 days! I cannot speak highly enough of him and recommend him to anyone for their future mortgage needs. Thank you Jake Taylor team!!

– Matthew Carey

****

"Jake is the mortgage guy you need to talk to when you are buying a home or looking to refinance you mortgage. Hands down Jake will walk you through the process and make sure you are getting the best possible deal. There are a lot of mortgage sharks out there so watch out!! Jake and his team know what banks have the best programs and can shop around your mortgage to make sure you are getting what's best."

— James Hansen

****

"I have nothing but great things to say about Jake. What started as a general conversation ended up with Jake helping me refinance my home. I was upside down on my home, in a bad ARM. Jake walked me through the process and we closed in less than a few weeks. The process was easy, effortless and efficient. Jake always is there for you, answering calls and emails. Moreover, Jake looked out for my best interests at every turn, saving me money on home insurance and also explaining things to me in great detail, letting me know all possible outcomes. Hire Jake, you will not regret it."

— Ben Fisher

****

"Jake and his team are true professionals. I have worked with Jake and his team for over 10 years, buying and then refinancing my home. Jake was able to secure a very competitive loan, but also gave me a sense of security knowing he and his team had my best interest at heart. They made the process painless and easy. I would recommend Jake to anyone."

– Steve Magnum

****

TABLE OF CONTENTS

About The Author

I'm a husband and father of four beautiful children, living in Arizona, and a graduate of ASU. I'm also a U.S. Army Veteran. I've been a mortgage broker since 2001, and have personally handled nearly 1,500 loans for my clients. The average amount I have helped homebuyers to finance is ~$12 million per year; throughout my career, I have helped borrowers gain access to over $200 million in loans.

Why Is Paying Off Your Mortgage Important?

Once I've helped someone finance the purchase of a home (or a refinance of their existing property), it's my goal to then help that person start paying off their mortgage faster and easier than they ever thought possible.

When people buy real estate, they don't realize that when they choose a bank to finance them, they're also choosing a business partner. My job is to help clients to choose the right partner to meet their needs.

Mortgages are similar to taxes, and no one likes paying taxes. No one **wants** to take out a mortgage. However, just as many people want to drive on smooth public roads and put their kids in top-notch school districts, people who want to own property often must partner with a bank borrow enough money to purchase the property they want.

When most folks first set out to buy a home, they rarely have the money available to pay 100% cash up front. They need a mortgage, with the end goal of owning the property free and clear "some day" in the future.

Banks are business partners to homeowners. As a mortgage professional, I act as an advocate for buyers looking to finance real estate through these bank partners.

In addition to serving as an advocate to help my clients choose the right bank partners, I also help them clearly understand how mortgages work. In fact, the whole goal of this book is to educate people on how to pay off their mortgage sooner, so you can experience financial freedom that much quicker.

CHAPTER 1

HOW DOES INTEREST & MORTGAGES WORK?

People may not be aware that their monthly mortgage payment is divided, where a percentage of their payment goes toward accumulated interest on their loan and the remainder towards their principle balance.

Let's say you have a $250,000 mortgage with a 6% interest rate for 30 years. In this example, your monthly mortgage payment will be $1,499, the majority of which ($1,250 of the

$1,499) will go towards paying the interest on the loan. In the first year of your payments, only $250 a month will go towards paying down your principle balance. Over a period of 30 years, you're going to pay off the entire principal ($250,000), but you're ALSO going to pay approx. $289,109 in interest!

The higher your mortgage's interest rate, the less principal you're paying in the initial portion of the loan. If you were start a 30 year loan today, depending on your interest rate, approx. 70 - 80% of your monthly payments would go toward interest, which goes straight into the pockets of the bank.

When you look at it on paper, this seems quite unfair. Why would anyone buy a home if they end up paying triple its price in the end for the privilege of borrowing money?

Would a bank lend you money in this case? Of course they would, because of the tremendous profit incentive!

THIS IS WHY I serve as the advocate and go-between with the bank and the borrower to minimize issues, get the best and lowest interest rates and repayment terms, and ensure my clients understand how and WHY to pay off their mortgages faster. (details to come shortly)

Why Pay Off Your Mortgage Faster?

Financial freedom comes when you start keeping and growing some of the money you make each month, instead of paying it all to expenses.

When your work and your paycheck exceeds your expenses, and you're above breakeven, you're on the road to financial freedom. For many people, a mortgage payment consumes a huge percentage of their paycheck.

If you are considering retiring in the next 15-20 years, you certainly don't want to be paying a mortgage and taxes when you do. Paying off your mortgage may help you to live the lifestyle you want to live when you get older, because eliminating your mortgage payment greatly reduces the amount of cash you need to meet your monthly expenses.

CHAPTER 2

WHAT IS MORTGAGE INSURANCE AND HOW DOES IT IMPACT MY LOAN?

Often people don't have the standard 20% down payment needed when purchasing a home to eliminate the requirement for mortgage insurance. When a borrower puts down less than 20% of the home's purchase price, the lending bank will require mortgage insurance to protect the lender from the homeowner defaulting on the loan, the property going to foreclosure auction, and the lender losing some or all of the money they lent the borrower to purchase the house.

After all, banks are certainly not in the business to lose money, and they have decided that they face a significant risk of not making money, tying up their capital for years, and losing money if a borrower defaults on a highly financed property. That's why they require mortgage insurance.

What Others Factors Influence Needing Mortgage Insurance and What Your Monthly Premiums Cost?

Lower down payment equals higher mortgage insurance rate due to higher risk from greater leverage. For example, if you put between zero and 5% down, your mortgage insurance premium rate will be higher than if you put 10-15% down. When you're required to have mortgage insurance, now your monthly payments will go to: 1) accumulated interest on your loan, 2) your mortgage insurance premium, and 3) finally, paying down your principle balance. (Note: we haven't even included property taxes, hazard insurance, HOA fees, and more. Ugh.)

The good news when paying mortgage insurance? You can escape its requirement well in ADVANCE of paying off your entire mortgage.

So by paying off your mortgage faster, not only do you save tens of thousands in interest payments, you also end your mortgage insurance requirement and premiums earlier.

For conventional loans, when your home equity is 22% or greater (meaning you owe less than 78% of the value of your home) you can drop your mortgage insurance altogether (automatically or by request, depending on your mortgage type).

Mortgage insurance premiums are also based on your credit score (higher score = lower default risk = lower premium), down payment percentage (higher DP = lower risk = lower premium) and loan amount.

Ex: a borrower has a 640 credit score and offers a 5% down payment on a $300,000 house. Their lender will likely require $180 a month in mortgage insurance premiums. (based on internal rate calculations - do not rely upon this number as accurate, please) However, if a borrower has a 750 credit score, puts 15% down and finances $300,000, the mortgage insurance could be only $85 each month. Note: these numbers vary greatly based on those several factors mentioned above.

The First Major Step Towards Paying Off Your Mortgage – Eliminating Mortgage Insurance

A good first milestone and step toward financial freedom is paying enough down your mortgage balance to allow you to drop the additional cost of mortgage insurance.

For example, once you reach 78% equity based on the original purchase price of your home (or if you believe your home has appreciated to provide you 22%+ equity, and you obtain a certified appraisal), you may (depending on your loan type) be able to call your bank to tell them you've reached this milestone and to remove your mortgage insurance requirement. Sometimes, mortgage insurance may drop off on its own, but never depend on your bank to catch this – reminding them the moment you can (for conventional or conforming loans) will often remove mortgage insurance.

Note: If you order an appraisal, you will often need to use a certified appraiser that your bank accepts. If your home's current appraised value shows that you have 22%+ equity, then you can drop your mortgage insurance.

There is another way to be rid of mortgage insurance as well… Instead of 'hoping' the value of your home increases enough to get rid of your mortgage insurance, or paying your monthly payments for years on end… you can accelerate this process (details soon to come).

Peeking ahead, once you no longer have to pay mortgage insurance, you can then put that extra money toward your payment every month and further accelerate the pay down and pay off of your mortgage towards the financial freedom finish line.

Going back to the factors that govern mortgage insurance premiums, remember that loans with smaller down payments generally come with higher interest rates.

Bonus: as you pay down your mortgage, as an additional possible reward and accelerant to paying it off, you also unlock more favorable interest rates if you refinance your loan, further reducing your monthly payment, and allowing you to put even more money towards paying off your mortgage in full.

Federal Housing Administration (FHA) Mortgage Insurance Rules

Borrowers who don't qualify for a conventional loan are often able to obtain an FHA loan instead. (loan requirements are easier to meet for FHA borrowers).

With an FHA loan, however, one tradeoff is that mortgage insurance (MI) is required for the life of the loan if you put less than 10% down. (if you put 10% down or more, your MI premium ends after 11 years)

FHA mortgage insurance premiums are more expensive, because the credit risk the consumer to the lender is higher, due to lower down payments, lower required credit scores, and other easier qualifications. This can be one reason that FHA loans are less favorable than conventional loans.

In order to remove these higher MI premiums before 11 years of payments (or before 30 years of payments when <10% down payment is made) you would have to refinance out of your FHA loan, which comes with a refi cost.

Let's say you start with a 5% down payment and you pay down your loan (or your property appreciates) so that you now have 10% equity; if interest rates are favorable, will it be financially better if you refinance out of your FHA into a conventional loan?

We live in a capitalistic economy, and current market conditions determine what the market rates will be at any given moment. (at one time, 30+ years ago, the prime rate for mortgages was over 12%) For example, let's assume interest rates are the same as when you originally took out your loan and you reach the milestone of 10% equity.

In this case, let's say your credit score has slightly improved as well so you can refinance (without pulling cash out) and your mortgage insurance premium decreases from $250 a month to $100 a month, saving you $100 a month.

If it costs you $3,000 in refinance fees, how long will it take you to 'earn back' the refi fees you paid and start profiting from a lower mortgage insurance premium?

This is a complicated calculation, and beyond the scope of this book, but something to consider when evaluating whether to refi your home to move from an FHA loan to another loan type, in the attempt to reduce or eliminate your mortgage insurance.

In some cases, you'll get a good ROI (return on investment) by doing this, and in some cases, you may not. Consult with a qualified lender first.

CHAPTER 3

WHAT IS A LENDER-LEVEL PRICING ADJUSTMENT?

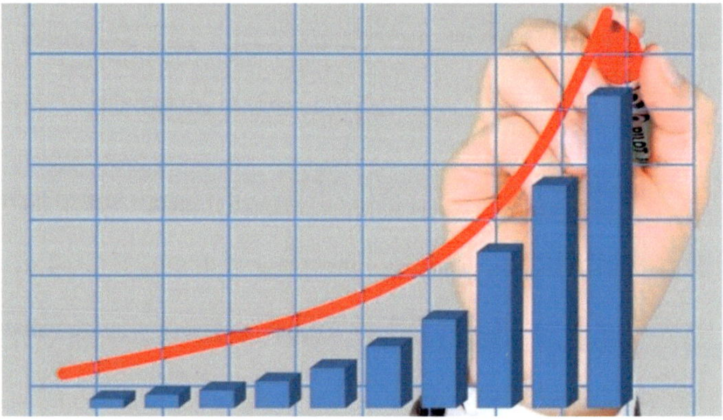

Lenders are all about managing and mitigating their risk when lending to borrowers. Another tool in your lender's toolbelt is known as a LLPA (Lender Level Pricing Adjustment).

In plain English, this means that the risker you are as a borrower in the eyes of the lender, the higher the interest rate they're going to charge you on your mortgage.

Riskier borrowers often make lower incomes, have higher debt-to-income ratios, have lower credit scores, have less money to put down on a home, spottier employment histories, and on and on.

For example, on a 95% LTV (loan-to-value) loan, meaning that the borrower is coming in with only a 5% down payment, a lender may charge 1.6% higher interest on a loan for borrowers with a 620 or less credit score, yet offer a 1.6% LOWER interest rate to a borrower with a 720+ credit score.

Another form of LLPA is when a lender (using this same borrower scenario as just described), may require a 3% fee (3% of the loan amount) for a low credit score borrower in order to "buy down" an artificially higher interest rate, vs. what was offered to a high credit score borrower. Ex: on a $200,000 loan, the low credit score borrower would pay a $6,000 buy down fee (3% of $200k) to get the same rate as the borrower with the high credit score. Fair? Not for me to say, but LLPAs exist and it's good to be aware of them.

So how can you avoid or minimize LLPA costs when financing a home? Be a stronger borrower; have a higher credit score; put more money down, etc, because lenders know that the default rates on mortgages are usually lower for people who are "stronger" borrowers.

Let's say you have 20% equity in your home (which is a great milestone) but all the sudden, you fall on financial hard times. Under these circumstances, you might miss a car payment, or start paying your credit card payments late.

But… no matter what, data shows that you're much more likely to prioritize paying your mortgage vs. other payments, especially when you have significant equity.

Ex: If you have $80,000 invested in your home based on 9 years of payments, and have repaired and maintained your home, raised kids and spent 9 years there, you're going to be very unwilling to lose your equity AND your place to live. Lenders know this, and that's why the more skin in the game you have when it comes to your house (equity, time in your house, and other factors), the better a risk you are.

This is why LLPA costs are lower, based on these positive indicators I've just described.

The Psychology of Equity, Time and Personal Investment in Your Home

People have a psychological, visceral connection to our homes. It's our "home" after all. We are living the American dream as we get closer and closer to eliminating our mortgages.

The banks know that as we pay down our mortgages, we become more connected to our homes and to our communities. They know the chance of defaulting on our loan goes down as we continually earn the right and ownership of our home. It's our own blood, sweat and tears that have gone into our property.

Banks know very well that homeowners are very reluctant to lose their property the longer they've lived there, and the more they've paid down their mortgage. Home equity is like cash in the bank.

The bottom line is, when it comes to buying a property or refinancing, the more equity you have or will have in your house, the better interest rates you can expect, due to lower lender risk.

When you have a better interest rate, your cash flow will increase and you will have more discretionary income to decide how you want to spend it (hopefully to pay your mortgage off sooner!)

Mortgage Payoff Milestones

The first beneficial milestone, when buying or owning a home, is to reach **10% equity**, either through down payment, paying down your mortgage, and a hopefully increase in your home's value.

10% equity is a welcome first milestone, because it will reduce your mortgage insurance premium (if you refinance or upon purchase with 10% down), making it cheaper to pay your monthly payments. 10% down payment also opens the door to easier refinance or purchase terms, and conventional or lower interest loans.

Having **15% equity** in your home is another positive milestone. There's a big difference between 90% vs. 85% LTV. Remember, at 78% LTV, your mortgage insurance premium goes away.

If you choose to do a straight refinance (no cash out, called a rate and term refinance) at 15% equity, you will likely get a lower interest, significantly cheaper mortgage insurance, and the freed up cashflow to pay down your remaining mortgage faster.

The next milestone of **20% equity** (20% upon purchase or 22% during ownership) removes your mortgage insurance requirement and opens the door to significantly lower interest rates on purchases and rate and term refinancing.

Better interest rates continue to accrue until you reach 40% equity in your home, and mentally, the more equity you have in your home, the more solid you'll feel financially, which will translate to all aspects of your life and confidence in yourself and financial future.

CHAPTER 4

COMMON MORTGAGE LOAN LENGTHS (AMORTIZATION) FOR RESIDENTIAL LOANS

Amortization is the amount of time your loan will be in effect, and the amount of time you must make payments on your loan to pay it off. Common amortization periods are 30 years and 15 years, although, by far, the most common loan length is a 30-year, fixed rate mortgage loan.

When you first finance a house purchase, you're taking a new loan and starting a 30 year repayment period. Some borrower, because they can tolerate higher monthly payments and are ambitious about paying off their mortgage, take 15 year loans. There are certain loan products that allow for 25, 20, 15, and 10-year loans, although they are less common than 30-year loans.

Before you purchase a home, or agree to a certain loan length, take into account how you're actually likely to make your payments. Are you committed to paying off your loan sooner than 30 years? Are you able to afford higher payments on a 15 year loan, or are you on the edge financially, where a minor downturn in the economy or loss of your job could prevent you from making your monthly payments?

There is no shame in honestly assessing your financial aptitude and habits to make the right, individual, person decision to accept a new loan or refinance for a certain loan term (ex: 30 years vs. 15 years).

There are typically two times when you must consider the length of your loan: 1) when you initially take out financing to buy a property, and 2) when you refinance.

The great thing is that there is nothing stopping you from paying off your loan faster than the amortization period you've chosen. You can, by paying the right amount, pay off a 30-year mortgage in 28, 25, or even 19 years if you choose. (but you will be in trouble if you try to lengthen the term of your repayment without working with your bank – i.e. missing payments!)

If you are someone whose natural instinct is to pay more than your monthly minimum payments, fantastic for you. Many people find it easier to have their lender tell them their minimum monthly payment based on their amortization schedule and interest rate. Most are not disciplined nor aggressive enough to pay extra on their mortgage… and that's totally ok.

Why Pay Your Mortgage Faster Than Your Amortization Period Calls For?

As mentioned previously, a 30-year mortgage loan, depending on your interest rate, will cost you the entire amount of your mortgage in interest, effectively doubling the price you pay for your home over 30 years (ex: a $200,000 loan at 5% interest will cost you $186,512 in interest over 30 years, in addition to repaying $200,000 in principle)

If you recoil at the thought of paying double (at least) for the house you just purchased, or the house you are currently paying on, then consider paying your mortgage off faster than 30 years to save yourself possibly tens of thousands of dollars in interest. We'll discuss specifics on how much to pay and when in the next chapter.

When Is The Best Time to Start Paying Your Mortgage Off Faster?

Once you reach 22% equity, not only can you drop your mortgage insurance requirement (except on an FHA loan with less than 10% down), at this milestone, you have the ability to do things like refinance for a shorter payback period (shorter amortization), which may increase your payments by a little, but will certainly help you pay off your mortgage faster.

Let's say you've paid down your 30 year mortgage, and your home has appreciated to give you 22%+ equity, it has taken you 7 years, and you decide to refinance. You can lower your payments by refinancing and taking out a new 30 year loan, but that's only going to delay you paying off your mortgage, and cost you EVEN MORE in interest over the next 30 years. Since you have 23 years left on your mortgage, you can either refinance and take a new 23 year loan, or perhaps you'll shorten it to a 20 year payback, or 15 years.

If you do this, you are going to see a higher mortgage payment each month, but, depending on prevailing interest rates, your payment may not be higher, or it may STILL be lower than before! In addition, you will pay less interest over the remaining life of the loan due to the shorter payback period.

If your goal is to pay off your loan faster but you know your discipline level is to only make the minimum payment your lender asks, then do yourself the favor, and at the very least, do not extend the length of your refinanced loan; shorten it if you can, as much as you can reasonably tolerate. Your future self will thank you!

Consider paying off your mortgage as a marathon, not a short race. When you're halfway through a marathon, you have less distance in front of you than you've already run, and this should hearten you to get you to the finish line. Now's not the time to run slower, it's the time to run a bit faster, to get to your goal sooner to enjoy the rewards at the end.

Taking advantage of lower interest rates, removing your mortgage insurance, and shortening your loan repayment period to save interest is the same thing. It makes paying off your house more achievable, tangible and within reach, time-wise.

Psychologically, it puts a spring in your step when you can see that loan balance shrinking every month. The closer you get to the finish line, the greater your pride of home ownership and the feeling of accomplishment.

How Fast Should You Accelerate Your Loan Payoff?

There are different ways to go about paying off your mortgage early. One way would be to save up money by investing, hoping that in a few years you will have enough to make a large, lump-sum payment against your mortgage in addition to paying it monthly.

For some people it helps having a safety net (a nest egg) that's separate from and not tied to their home equity, in the event real estate values drop.

If real estate values decrease, it may dishearten you that you've paid so much into your home, only to have your equity diminished, so you have to decide how aggressively you're going to pay down and pay off your mortgage.

If you have invested outside of your home in addition to paying it, at least you have additional money in your retirement or savings account that you can use in an emergency situation, or in case real estate values drop close to when you're going to sell your home and/or retire.

Please remember that this book is not financial or tax advice, and to consult with a qualified professional when making any financial decision.

CHAPTER 5

COMMON-SENSE, SIMPLE WAYS TO PAY OFF YOUR MORTGAGE YEARS IN ADVANCE AND SAVE TENS OF THOUSANDS IN INTEREST

There are many strategies for paying off your mortgage early. An important question to ask yourself is: "How much can I comfortably afford to put toward my mortgage every month without running into financial difficulty, and what happens if my money situation deteriorates suddenly?"

Sometimes, the best-laid plans of mice and men often go awry (this means that life happens, and often, unexpected events can change your life significantly and quickly).

Here Are Few Fast-Mortgage-Payoff Examples:

1. Let's say you are a salaried employee, and you decide to make 1/12 of an extra payment every month ($1432 / mo divided by 12 months = $119.33 extra per month) on a $300,000 loan at a rate of 4% over 30 years. By paying the 1/12 of an extra payment every month on this loan, you would pay off your mortgage 4 years and 1 month sooner, saving you $33,315 dollars in interest over the life of the loan.

   If you made the one extra payment all at once instead of paying it in pieces monthly, you would pay off your mortgage 4 years earlier instead of four years and one month earlier.

2. If you made 2 extra payments a year (being more aggressive), you would pay off your loan 7 years earlier and save over $50,000 of interest.
3. Right now, the average purchase price my clients pay for a home is $400,000. If you put 5% down ($20,000) and finance the remaining $380,000 at 4% interest, and your goal is to rid yourself of the scourge of mortgage insurance as soon as possible…

   …by making your minimum monthly payments only, you would reach a $312,000 loan amount (putting you at the 22% equity mark, assuming no appreciation) after 104 payments, or just under nine years, at which time you could ask your lender to remove your mortgage insurance requirement.

Using this example, let's say you made one extra payment a year or an additional 1/12 of a payment each month. This would get you to the $312,000 mark, where you could drop the mortgage insurance after 84 months instead of 104 months, saving yourself nearly two years of mortgage insurance payments. If your mortgage insurance payments were $200 a month, this would mean a savings of $200 * 12 months = $2,400 a year alone.

4. The last scenario we will look at is really aggressive but worth having a look at. If you pay one extra payment a quarter, it will save 11 years on your mortgage. Paying your mortgage at this accelerated rate can remove can your mortgage insurance in four years instead of nearly 9 years. This will also allow you to pay off your mortgage in 19 years vs. 30 years, and save you approximately $100,000 in interest!

    Think of it this way. For the price of a luxury vehicle lease, you could pay off your mortgage 11 years earlier and be financially "free-er". "Mortgage free" is the new BMW status symbol.

What Does It Feel Like to Pay Off Your Mortgage?

When you pay off your mortgage, it's like being released from debtors 'prison. Clients tell me that the feeling is pure freedom. With no lifestyle or income change, they are looking at approximately $1,800 - $2,700 extra a month in their pocket. Paying off a mortgage is almost like retiring early. Instead of paying the bank each month, your money is just sitting in your checking account or wherever you choose to keep it.

Regardless of what anyone ever tells you about the tax consequence of paying off a mortgage, you are still getting taxed at probably a 50% rate. So really, it's like a $3,600 to $5,400 a month pay increase. Think about that. Even though you may a bit extra in taxes, due to the lack of mortgage interest paid, you're still several thousand dollars a month richer.

Start Paying Off Your Mortgage NOW by Contacting Jake Taylor at Pilot Mortgage

At Pilot Mortgage, we not only handle a wide range of loans for our clients, we help our clients throughout the years of owning their homes with fast mortgage pay-down strategies, as you've read in this book.

We handle reverse mortgages for seniors, FHA loans, USDA loans for those buying in rural areas, Veterans (VA) loans and conventional / conforming loans. We can also help finance Jumbo loans, if needed.

We also help self-employed people to acquire financing, and can sometimes qualify people using bank statement or stated income loans, or for people buying investment properties, and we also handle commercial loans (though this is not the core of our business). If there's a property with a commercial use or a residential use I will make a loan on that property.

To take the first steps towards paying your mortgage off years sooner than you thought and to save tens of thousands in interest, or to obtain financing or refinance your home:

Visit: JakeTaylor.com

Text me: (480) 999-3339

NOTES

Made in the USA
Monee, IL
05 November 2026

67385072R00033